NORTH AMERICAN INDIAN WOMEN

NORTH AMERICAN INDIAN WOMEN

ROBIN LANGLEY SOMMER

JG PRESS

Published in the USA 1998 by JG Press
Distributed by World Publications, Inc.

The JG Press imprint is a trademark of
JG Press, Inc.
455 Somerset Avenue
North Dighton, MA 02764

Produced by
Brompton Books Corporation
15 Sherwood Place
Greenwich, CT 06830

ISBN 1-57215-159-5

Printed in China

PAGE 1: Navajo textile by contemporary
weaver Rita Nez Begay.

PAGE 2: The Pottery Dance, still
performed by Zuñi women, celebrates
their historic role as water carriers
from springs far below the pueblo.

OPPOSITE: A classic Edward S. Curtis
photograph of a Northwest Coast elder
with her handiwork – a basket woven
with striking diagonals and the image
of a horse.

Photo Credits

Courtesy Karen Abeita: 75.
Alaska Division of Tourism, Department of Commerce & Economic Development,
Juneau, AK: 121.
American Museum of Natural History, New York, NY: 80, 100; Photograph by Adam
Anik: 25, 113; Photograph by Denis Finnin: 62; Photograph by Kerry Perkins: 37.
The Bettmann Archive: 18, 76–77 (all four), 78, 79, 117.
Blitz Antique Native American Art Ltd., Crompond, NY, Photograph by Charles
Bechtold: 26, 29, 72.
Courtesy W. E. Channing and Co., Santa Fe, NM, Photograph by Addison Doty: 112.
Courtesy The Creek Nation: 93.
Courtesy Cristof's, Santa Fe, NM, Photograph by Pamela Nicosin: 92; Photograph by
Mark Nohl: 1, 69, 73, 115, 127.
Courtesy Cristof's and the Santa Fe Collection: 116.
Charles Donaldson Native American Art, Scottsdale, AZ, Photograph by Al Costanzo:
22.
The Halpern Collection, Courtesy J. Mark Sublette/Medicine Man Gallery, Tucson,
AZ, Photograph by Robin Stancliff: 101.
The John Hopkins University, Special Collections, The Milton S. Eisenhower Library,
Baltimore, MD: 14, 31, 36, 41, 87, 98.
Kenji Kawano: 2, 52, 109, 122.
Leo Kim: 125 (bottom right).
Library of Congress: 10, 40, 45, 90, 94.
Medical College of Pennsylvania, Archives and Special Collections on Women in
Medicine: 17.
Minnesota Historical Society Museum Collections, St. Paul, MN, Photograph by Peter
Latner: 54; Donated by Jeannette and Harry Ayer (by Lattner): 57.
Courtesy Morning Star Gallery, Santa Fe, NM, Photograph by Addison Doty: 15, 16,
23, 28, 34, 38, 55, 56 (both), 63, 64, 65, 66, 67, 81, 86, 102, 103.
National Anthropological Archives, Smithsonian Institution, Washington, DC: 6, 8, 9,
21, 32, 33, 47, 49, 50, 51, 53, 59, 74, 88, 89, 91, 96, 99, 107, 111, 119, 120.
National Archives: 7, 58, 118.
National Museum of the American Indian, Smithsonian Institution, New York, NY:
27, 105.
New Mexico Tourism and Travel Division, Commerce & Industry Department, Santa
Fe, NM: 48, 126.
Courtesy Oklahoma Indian Art Gallery, Oklahoma City, OK: 106.
Peabody Essex Museum, Salem, MA, Photograph by Mark Sexton: Collected by John
Cochrane, Collection of Millicent Nichols: 60; Donated by L. C. Hurd: 68.
The Picture Cube: David Ball: 95, 97; Gene Peach: 12, 110.
Reuters/Bettmann Newsphotos: 24.
Gail Russell: 123.
San Diego Museum of Man, CA, Photograph by Ken Hedges: 46, 104.
Courtesy Second Phase Gallery, Taos, NM: 70, 71 (bottom).
Christopher Selser, Santa Fe, NM, Photograph by Herb Lotz, Santa Fe, NM: 71 (top),
85.
Smithsonian Institution, Washington, DC: 30, 35.
Tennessee State Library and Archives: 19 (top right).
University of Washington Libraries, Special Collections, Seattle, WA: 5, 42, 43, 84,
108.
UPI/Bettmann Newsphotos: 11, 19 (bottom left), 39, 44, 61, 83, 114, 124, 125 (top left).

CONTENTS

INTRODUCTION

Since paleo-Indian times, North American Indian women have held a central place in the life of their tribes, honored as the bringers of new life, sustainers of the people through many skillful tasks, teachers, healers, spiritual leaders, and revered elders. From childhood, Indian girls were taught to carry out their work with pride in their contribution to community life. There were, and are, time-honored rituals connected with food gathering, agriculture, cooking, dressing meat and hides, making clothes for everyday use and for ceremonies, building shelters, and many other skills passed on by example, instruction, and storytelling.

Like children everywhere, Indian girls had toys that helped prepare them for their future responsibilities: dolls and small cradleboards, miniature tipis and cooking utensils, "ponies" made of forked sticks. Objects like the kachina dolls of the Pueblo people taught them about their spiritual heritage. Family and community life were inseparable, and all members of the tribe contributed in some way to the development of the children. Close ties of affection were the norm, and the extended family looked after its own. In some tribes, it was the uncle rather than the father who saw a boy through the rites of passage into adult life. For girls, it was their mothers, grandmothers, aunts, and other female elders. Children of both sexes were highly valued, safeguarded, and led gradually through the maturation process, with time for play and exercise.

Because Indian women were brought up to be physically strong and to divide the labor with the men of the tribe, early European observers who knew nothing about Native American culture believed

RIGHT: A Dakota woman and her daughter in traditional dress, ornamented with dentalium shells and silver concha belts, c. 1904.

LEFT: A Hopi girl of marriageable age assumes the traditional squash-blossom hairstyle, symbolizing fertility.

they were mistreated beasts of burden. The word "squaw" – a corruption of the Narragansett word for woman – embodied that misperception. In fact, these women were highly respected and carried out essential roles. While the men of the tribe defined themselves largely by hunting and warfare, especially in the East and on the Plains, they were not rigid about gender roles. Women could take on male responsibilities if they wished and serve as scouts, hunters, mediators, and even warriors, especially to avenge the death of a husband or brother.

There was also autonomy unknown to European cultures in the fact that most Indian women retained control of the goods they brought into mar-

riage and had the right to space their pregnancies. They were rarely forced to marry against their will, and divorce could sometimes be obtained simply by placing a husband's personal effects outside the dwelling. If there was mistreatment, a woman's relatives came to her assistance and mediated between the couple.

In most societies, menarch was the dividing line between girlhood and womanhood. It was publicly acknowledged, often by a period of ritual separation, and ushered in new rites of adolescence. Among the Tlingit, the father gave a potlatch, or ceremonial distribution of gifts, and wealthy clans sequestered their girls for as long as two years – it was a proof of status. Cheyenne fathers gave away a valuable horse when their daughters reached maturity. Kumeyaay elders tattooed a girl's face, and Salish mothers made an

enveloping "virgin cape" to conceal their daughters' bodies from masculine eyes. A Hopi adolescent adopted the traditional "squash blossom" hairstyle to show that she was of marriageable age and was allowed to meet her suitor at an appointed trysting place near the pueblo.

Some tribes were vigilant about a young woman's chastity, among them the Papago, the Kootenay, the Apache, and the Plains peoples. Premarital sex was punished, and girls married young to ensure their virginity. Other tribes allowed greater sexual freedom. Some Pueblo groups encouraged young couples who intended marriage to sleep together, and illegitimacy was not a stigma. Unmarried Natchez women competed for gifts and attention from young men of the tribe and brought these gifts to their marriages as dowries.

Courtship rituals varied from those of the Iroquois, in which a man asked permission of a girl's parents and gave her a wampum ornament to invite a trial marriage, to those of the Ojibwa, where a young woman sang special songs to attract the man of her choice, or hired a medicine woman to sing them for her. Kiowa men of the Plains invited young women to stand beside them, enveloped in their wearing blankets, for private conversation. But most marriages were arranged by the girl's family. They were not expected to be love matches, although the girl could refuse if she chose. The dominant factors in marriage and community life were the kinship system and the culture's means of subsistence.

Generally speaking, the tribes east of the Mississippi reckoned kinship matrilineally – through the female line – and subsisted mainly on the products of female agriculture. Women's influence was especially high among those cultures that included the tribes of the Iroquois League – Seneca, Cayuga, Mohawk, Onondaga, and Oneida – the Algonquians of the mid-Atlantic coast, and the southeastern woodlands peoples, including the Cherokee, Chickasaw, Creek, and Natchez (most of whom were eventually forced to relocate farther west to so-called Indian Territory). For the most part, these tribes lived in permanent villages surrounded by fields of staple crops, including corn, squash, and beans, and traced descent through the female line. Married couples generally lived with the wife's family (matrilocally).

The Iroquois way of life, in what is now New York State, was typical of a matrilineal society prior to the arrival of the Europeans. Each maternal lineage group, known as an *ohwachira*, collectively owned the tribe's principal property: longhouses, fields, tools, seeds, dried foods, and burial grounds. In the case of divorce, the husband left the household and children to the support of the community. Social and ceremonial life centered on agriculture, and three female societies presided over the annual rituals: the Sisters of the Three Life Sustainers, the Society of the Women Planters, and the Sisters of the Life Supporters.

Among the Plains and central prairie tribes of the 18th and 19th century, women had less authority, commensurate with the importance of game animals hunted by men. Most of these tribes practiced some agriculture, but they depended more heavily on game pursued during seasonal migrations than on crops. The Pawnee, of present-day Nebraska, are an example. The men lived with their wives' families in earth-lodge villages during the spring planting and fall harvest seasons, but followed the buffalo and lived in tipis winter and summer. Then the community divided along male kinship lines, with activity focused on the hunters and their needs.

A similar nomadic lifestyle, but more pronounced, prevailed on the Great Plains among the buffalo-hunting Lakota and Dakota (Sioux), Cheyenne, Comanche, Crow, Blackfeet, and Gros Ventre. Migration was a way of life, and the few tools and household utensils they crafted were frequently left behind, to be replaced at the next encampment. The women produced no pottery, as it was not

BELOW: A Cheyenne family moves camp via travois, with the youngest child in a cradleboard.

readily portable, and basket weaving was little practiced for lack of suitable native plants. The girls of these tribes were skilled horsewomen, who had been riding since early childhood.

In the arid Southwest, both farming and hunting were precarious, and the diverse tribes of this area evolved several ways of life. The Zuñi, Hopi, and Pueblo peoples traced their origins to the Anasazi, or Old Ones, who built their cliff villages here long before recorded history. They farmed the flood plains of the Rio Grande and its tributaries, and the arroyos below the mesas on which they built their own villages. Water was collected in cisterns or carried up from ground level by the women, who balanced their *ollas*, or jars, on their heads with rings made of fiber. Women also helped farm the tribal fields, which belonged to them and descended through matrilineal lines. Fertility was at the heart of both material and spiritual life.

The Navajo arrived in the Southwest about A.D. 1500 and developed a seminomadic way of life centered on their flocks of sheep and goats, owned by the women and tended primarily by them. The Navajo adopted many farming techniques from the Pueblo tribes, who also taught them how to weave the cotton they used for clothing. Navajo women became famous for their skill at weaving blankets, rugs, and clothing from the wool of their flocks and from commercial yarns obtained from traders during the 19th century. The men learned silversmithing from the Spanish and made beautiful jewelry and belts called *conchas* incorporating local stones like turquoise, worn by both sexes not only for ornament but also in the form of fertility charms and other amulets.

Six distinct Southwestern tribes comprise the Apache, who originally ranged from western Oklahoma through Arizona, Texas, and northern Mexico. The men hunted and raided neighboring tribes and white settlements for provisions and livestock, while the women gathered food: the division of labor was more distinct than in the sedentary tribes. Even so, women held a high status, as seen in the elaborate female puberty ceremonies of the Apache and the fact that the men owed primary allegiance to their wives' families. Produce gathered by Apache women included prickly pears, acorns (made into flour, as in California), piñon nuts, yucca fruit, mesquite beans, wild onions, berries, and cactus fruit. Girls were taught the same survival skills as boys, including riding, tracking, and self-defense with bow and arrow, knife, and rifle. They always kept a bundle of food and weapons at hand in case of an enemy raid that would throw them upon their own resources. They also crafted hide clothing decorated with beadwork and fringed leggings that were attached to moccasins and tied at the knee to protect the wearer's legs from the harsh desert vegetation.

On the Pacific Coast, most California tribes were headed by men and women had less influence.

Upon marriage, they lived with their husbands' families and served principally as stewards rather than owners of tribal goods. Their essential role was as gatherers, especially of the acorns that were their staple food. Women of these tribes, including the Maidu, Pomo, Hupa, and Modoc, became the finest basketmakers in the Americas, utilizing such materials as spruce root, fern, reeds, and willow. They also made wicker cradles lined with foxskin and elaborate ear ornaments crafted of feathers, bone, shells, and wampum. They even developed a form of watertight basket that could be used for cooking by dropping hot stones into the water. Thus they made porridge from

BELOW: An Apache woman hoes corn with her infant secured in the cradleboard on her back.

the acorns that they pounded into flour.

Tribes of the bleak Plateau area between the Rocky Mountains and the Sierra Nevada included the Paiute, southern Shoshone, and western Ute. Here, too, the people subsisted mainly upon seeds, nuts, and berries, as the area was too dry for farming and game was scarce. Women of these tribes collected piñon nuts, primrose seeds, and edible roots at their various encampments, while the men hunted rabbits, antelope, and deer. Most of their shelters were temporary *wickiups*, made of brush, reeds, or matting and readily portable.

In the Northwest, where food was abundant and easily obtained, an elaborate clan system evolved, in which the wealthiest families formed a kind of nobility. Women in these tribes, including the Tlingit of coastal Alaska and the Chinook of the Columbia River Valley, derived their status from relationship to clan headmen or their family's wealth, in the form of natural resources, heirloom objects, and the right to names and animal crests represented by the tribal totem poles. In turn, these women brought ancestral rank and privileges to their husbands when they married. Chilkat women used mountain-goat hair to weave blankets with animal designs in colors of

black, yellow, blue, and green. Basketmaking was an important skill, and both baskets and blankets were woven of cedar and decorated with traditional symbols, including the whale, bear, raven, and owl. Northwestern women were known for their culinary skills and prepared lavish feasts for the potlatch ceremonies for which they also produced many objects, including cedar storage chests, blankets, mats, and quillwork. Many families owned slaves, captured from other tribes, who did much of the heavy work and increased the family's status.

Healing was a function ascribed to women of most cultures, both as herbalists and shamans, or medicine women. Natural and supernatural elements were always involved, as illness was regarded as having a spiritual component: a malevolent entity within the body – the province of shamans – or an imbalance that could be corrected by the use of herbal and other natural remedies. Wounds were also treated with prescribed prayers and rituals as well as dressings and medicines. Among some tribes, women performed ritual prayers and actions throughout the period when the men were away on war parties or raids to keep them safe.

Women were often identified as healers when they experienced

ABOVE: Cheyenne women participate in the Buffalo Dance ceremony, a healing ritual performed in horned headdresses.

dreams or visions calling them to that role – a phenomenon that was universally respected. Among the Plains tribes, smoking played a part in healing rituals, due to the Lakota belief that the prayer pipe conferred upon the people by the spirit envoy White Buffalo Calf Woman put them into harmony with the universe. A woman has always represented this revered personage at the Sun Dance ceremony. Other tribes, too, centered rituals of peace and healing on pipe smoking, and sacred pipes are among the oldest artefacts that have come down from ancient cultures.

Navajo girls are believed to be suffused with healing power, the legacy of the primordial Changing Woman, during their four-day coming-of-age ceremony, the Kinaalda. Women of the Mescalero Apache perform a ritual function when they harvest the mescal crowns from the century plant and roast the harvest for tribal use. Similarly, Papago women of the Sonoran Desert, led by a grandmother, harvest the red fruit of the giant saguaro cactus to make ritual wine for the New Year rainmaking ceremonies.

Pomo women have always been revered as healers of the people, whether instructed by their elders or called by visions from the spirit world. Among the Cheyenne, mature women took part in the healing ceremony called the Massaum as Buffalo Dancers, wearing the traditional horned headdress. And Ojibwa women of the upper Midwest could win admittance to the revered Midewiwim, the Grand Medicine Society, through a long apprenticeship.

Among the Blackfeet, a medicine woman's buckskin bundle might contain more than a dozen roots and herbs, including snakeroot, for snakebite; trillium, for heart problems and gynecological disorders; juniper, used as a diuretic; muskrat root, for sore throat; and sumac root, for toothache. Healing implements used by the Crow included a sucking tube with which the medicine woman drew out the evil spirits causing the illness. Crow women were also members of the Tobacco Society, whose Medicine Dance ritual included planting the sacred tobacco in secret garden plots. Inuit healers used wormwood leaves, either chewed or brewed into tea, to relieve congestion and other cold symptoms.

The Comanche believed that a woman called to be an "eagle doctor" by a vision quest in adolescence came into the fullness of her powers only after menopause. Such was the case with the renowned 20th-century healer Sanapia, who used such potent charms as the tail feather of a golden eagle to heal those afflicted by deep physical and spiritual disorders, including the dreaded "ghost sickness." This paralyzing condition was believed to be caused by restless spirits of the dead, and severe cases required the ritual consumption or application of the drug peyote and prayers to both the Medicine Eagle, Sanapia's spiritual patron, and the Holy Spirit of the Judaeo-Christian Bible.

A common thread linking Native cultures across the land is respect for the elders of the community, with their great store of wisdom and

RIGHT: Seneca elder Nancy Blacksquirrel Miller, photographed in 1927. She remained well and active on New York's Tonawanda Reservation, near Buffalo, to well over 100 years of age.

endurance. Elderly women are honored as transmitters of tribal culture and a link between past and future generations: Mothers of the People. In recent decades, they have played a larger political part as well, serving on tribal councils and forming cooperatives for the sale of traditional products. The women's auxiliary of the Kiowa Tonkonga (Black Legs) warrior society carries on the tradition of the tribe's Old Women Society, historically consulted by warriors planning raids and returning from battle.

Among central California's Kashaya Pomo, the honored healer and prophet Essie Parrish, born in 1902 and raised largely by her maternal grandmother, served as spiritual

leader of her tribe from 1943 until 1979. She presided over the traditional Dance House ceremonies that invoked divine protection, and admitted women to the ranks of the Big Head Dancers, with their magnificent feathered headdresses. Parrish had succeeded another *maru*, or dreamer, named Annie Jarvis as spiritual leader of the Kashaya, but she moved away from Jarvis's isolationist policy to work with anthropologists, filmmakers, and linguists who wanted to preserve knowledge of Kashaya culture in the face of the tribe's dwindling numbers.

Among the female spirits who figure so largely in Indian spirituality is the Shawnee's Grandmother, who helped the Great Spirit create

humankind after a primordial flood. She still watches over her people from a celestial bark house, guiding them through the rituals that she ordained. The Bread Dance is one of the major ceremonies performed for Our Grandmother to ensure crops and fertility, and it is believed that the Grandmother's voice is sometimes heard joining those of the people in the traditional songs.

The Cherokee honored Selu, the Corn Giver, at the annual Green Corn Ceremony, in which women carried baskets of the season's first vegetables. Each of the seven clans has historically been represented by a spokeswoman, pre-eminent among whom was the Beloved Woman, through whom the Great Spirit spoke. Her emblem in Cherokee art is the swan's wing.

The matrilineal Mandan had a society of women elders who performed buffalo-calling rites during the winter months to lure the herds close to the village. Called the White Buffalo Society, it had a counterpart in the middle-aged women's group known as the Goose Society, which was devoted to rainmaking and the ensurance of good crops in the tribe's upper Missouri River homeland.

Traditionally, Indian women remain active in their communities into advanced old age, caring for the children, teaching traditional lore and skills, healing, and doing the daily tasks they learned from their own elders.

The rituals of mourning and bereavement were an important part of all Native American cultures, whether the dead were cremated, buried, or consigned to scaffolds, as on the Great Plains. A woman who had been widowed usually mourned her spouse for at least a year. Some Plains tribeswomen cropped off their hair, wailed, and cut their bodies to ensure a safe journey for their husbands to the afterlife. The Cheyenne, Arapaho, and Blackfeet burned the family tipi and dispersed its furnishings. In Mandan cemeteries two feathered offering poles were planted in a circle of human skulls, flanked by the skulls of a male and female buffalo. Ojibwa widows retained a spirit bundle filled with their husbands' effects until the end of their mourning period, when the bundle was consigned to his relatives. The Snohomish erected wooden grave houses over the coffins of their dead, and many tribes had customs whereby newborn children were named for the most recently deceased relative. In the Northwest, women rubbed ashes on their faces as a sign of mourning and wore special hats that signified their widowhood. But in almost every case, women of child-bearing age were expected to marry again and take up the tasks that were essential to the welfare of the community.

BELOW: At San Ildefonso Pueblo, New Mexico, the Corn Dance, performed in September, celebrates the harvest of the tribe's essential food.

Ethnologists have pointed out that American Indian languages have no words for either religion or art. Spirituality so pervaded everyday life and its customs and artefacts that there was no thought of making discrete entities of these activities. Broadly speaking, everything not only had a spirit but *was* spirit manifested in physical form – people, animals, plants, mountains and rivers, all of nature. Women's intimate connection to nature, with its seasonal cycles, fertility, and eternal renewal of life, is seen in the prayers, ceremonies, and legends of almost every tribe. The Pueblo people honor the female spirit as Mother Earth. The Iroquois call her Sky Woman. For the Inuit, she is Sedna; for the Cherokee, Selu, the giver of corn. The Lakota ascribe their seven holy rites, from the Sacred Pipe to memorial gift-giving on the anniversary of death, to White Buffalo Calf Woman, and it is believed that she will reappear among her people in the form of a white calf from the sacred herd still tended on the plains of South Dakota.

The most important event of the Zuñi calendar is the Shalako Ceremony, in which young women represent the six Corn Maidens who first transformed the field grasses into corn of many colors. Sent by the Sun, they return each year to bless the crop and sanctify the food to the use of the people. Pueblo girls carry ears of corn and pine boughs, symbolic of eternal life, while performing the ceremonial dance. Their colorfully dyed eagle-feather headdresses symbolize the sunlight, clouds, and rainbows that produce a good harvest. At Soyal, the Hopi New Year, the masked dancer who personates the kachina Ahulani (Corn Spirit) is accompanied by his sisters, Yellow Corn Girl and Blue Corn Girl. They celebrate at the winter solstice, as the sun slowly returns from its southern migration.

Navajo devotion to Changing Woman fuses the concepts of female fertility and that of the crops that sustain life. Sand paintings for the Blessingway ceremony show Changing Woman standing between stalks of corn above a cross that symbolizes Mother Earth. Generated by the Sun God, she created the Navajo after her twin sons, Monster Slayer and Child Born of Water, had cleared the world of demonic forces.

Ceremonial artefacts made by women are imbued with the faith heritage of the people. Many of the symbols that appear on ceremonial clothing and other objects can be traced to prehistoric mounds and petroglyphs: animal forms, human hands, linked scrolls, geometric figures, sunflowers, skybands (stepped figures), and cross-shaped elements representing the four directions of the compass, collectively, the earth. Dolls and animal fetishes of ancient lineage are still carefully guarded as part of the medicine bundle that confers personal and tribal power. Tribes including the Arikara appoint honored women to serve as Keeper of the Medicine Bundle.

Most ceremonial regalia, apart from the wooden masks used by the Northwestern and Alaskan tribes, was made by women, many of whom belonged to special guilds in which prayer and visions dictated the form or decoration of an object. Plains tribeswomen made special shirts, buffalo robes, dance sticks, and medicine bags decorated with quills and beads obtained from traders. Some held the exclusive right to paint or work certain designs used for honorary robes and other sacred objects. Occasionally, a woman who went to war, like Minnie Hollow Wood, who fought the U.S. Cavalry, won the right to wear the eagle-feather war bonnet.

Arikara women of North Dakota collected bundles of brush to build ceremonial lodges for tribal dances, even after they were confined to reservations and their customs were opposed by federal Indian agents. When the Hidatsa were removed to the Fort Berthold Reservation in 1882, Buffalo Bird Woman preserved the gardening lore and rituals of her tribe's Goose Society despite government efforts to make agriculture a male domain. Blackfeet holy women preserved their elk-hide Sun Dance robes throughout the fifty-year period (from 1883) when many tribal customs were outlawed as "heathenish rites."

Kiowa women still participate in the tribe's annual Gourd Dance, held to renew its spirit and prosperity. They also make special robes to honor the dead in their role as an auxiliary to the Warrior Society. Pueblo women paint the *tablitas* (headdresses) they wear in the Corn Dance, and sacred Navajo symbols are woven into the tribe's blankets and rugs. Shields, dresses, and shirts like those produced for the Ghost Dance ritual of the late 1800s were made to protect the wearers from enemy bullets and arrows by spiritual power. Yurok women of California underwent painful initiation rites to become healers – one of the few traditional paths to power among the California tribes.

Women of the Northwest Coast had a limited role in ceremonials, which consisted primarily of masked dancing by men, who personated totemic animals. Transformational magic played a predominant role in the spiritual life of these cultures. In parts of Washington State and Oregon, women took the leading role in the First Food ceremony, which followed the harvesting of nourishing roots gathered by female elders. Male drummers and bell ringers still participate in such gathering ceremonies among the Yakima and other Plateau tribes, but village families are not free to collect their own roots until the First Food ceremony has been carried out.

Standards of female beauty varied from tribe to tribe, and there were many different customs of ornamentation. Among the Kwakiutl, until the early 20th century, an elongated head was considered a mark of beauty, linked to a creation story in which the first man took a woman with a long head for a wife. Cowlitz women padded the skulls of their infant daughters and fashioned head- and footboards for their cradleboards that exerted continuous pressure, causing the forehead to become elongated. Wisham women wore nose ornaments of dentalium shell, which was highly prized all along the Pacific Coast, and heavily beaded hair ornaments, necklaces, and clothing. Yupik women of southern Alaska wore delicate bead and shell ornaments in their pierced ears, noses, and lower lips. During the 19th century, elaborate facial tattooing and body paint were worn by Mojave women to indicate their family and status. In other tribes, ornamentation was confined to jewelry made of metal, shell, bone, coral,

LEFT: This Wishham tribeswoman wears the dentalium shell nose ornament and the shell and bead jewelry that show her family's wealth and status.

bread and the kilns in which they fired pottery.

Seminole women of southern Florida presided over the traditional open-sided house called a *chickee* with its thatched roof and platform floor raised several feet above the ground. They spent many hours gathering and grating the roots of the wontie plant – a palmlike vegetable added to corn soup as a thickener. Corn kernels were pounded into meal in a hollowed log and used to make bread, soup, drinks, and other dishes. When hand-operated sewing machines reached the Everglades in the late 1800s, they expedited development of the multicolored patchwork clothing that became distinctive of the tribe.

Navajo women have been herding their sheep on ancestral lands for generations, sometimes traveling miles each day to reach pastureland and water. Like shepherds everywhere, they are especially busy during the lambing season, when orphaned lambs have to be bottle-fed several times a day. They also help construct the hogan, a dome-shaped dwelling of earth, stone, and timber. Weaving is a skill passed from mother to daughter and entails mastery of the skills that precede loomwork: shearing, carding the wool, and spinning it into yarn. Thick yarn is used for saddle blankets, medium-thick for rugs, and thin for tapestries. During the 19th century, trade items including Germantown yarn, red bayeta, and aniline dyes came into use to meet the demand for Navajo wearing blankets and rugs. More recently, tribeswomen have revived the use of dyes drawn from nature. The herb madder produces peach tones; ripe cactus fruit, pinks; walnut shells, browns; juniper berries, snakeweed, and wild carrot, yellows; and the indigo plant, blues. The plant called Navajo tea, used to color wool orange or gold, is handled reverently, like all wild herbs, which are considered gifts from the original Navajo Holy People. Whether pictorial or geometric designs are employed for weaving, they reflect the Navajo principles of balance and harmony.

and other materials, along with trade goods including buttons, tin cones, ribbons, glass beads, and cloth.

Among the people of coastal Alaska, carved masks and fetishes, historically made by men, dominated ceremonial life; daily life was family-centered and oriented toward survival in a harsh environment. Seal meat and fish were staple foods, supplemented by gathering during the brief summer months. It is only in recent years that Aleut women like Denise Wallace have begun to carve marine ivory. Wallace fashions scrimshawed fossil ivory into contemporary jewelry set in silver and gold, with native stones like lapis lazuli and lace agate.

Faithful performance of her daily tasks, from collecting firewood and water to building shelters, farming and gathering, and making clothing

and household utensils, brought honor to a woman and her family. The fact that many of these tasks were laborious and exhausting did not lessen, but increased, the prestige of Indian women. As Joseph Nicollet, an astute scientist-explorer, wrote after living among the Ojibwa during the early 1800s, the situation was one of mutual dependence and respect between the sexes, "not a matter of one sex having power over the other."

The household was pre-eminently the female domain, but men and women sometimes worked together to build their homes. Pueblo men put up the walls and roof beams, while women plastered the walls with adobe and covered the roof with grass, brushwood, and mud. They also made the beehive-shaped adobe oven (*horno*) in which they baked

Among the tribes of the Rocky Mountain region, the Apsaroke, or Crow, were widely considered exceptional for their hardiness and courage, including the women. They could carry heavy loads of slaughtered buffalo meat and ride all night with raiding war parties. During the winter, they encamped in tipis along cold mountain streams, and in the summer months they lived in large lodges and produced well-made clothing and beautiful horse trappings that were the envy of other tribes. Crow women were exceptionally skillful in beadwork, producing moccasins, cradleboards, and rifle cases with multicolored geometric designs outlined in white. Crow women also painted buffalo hides, a practice more commonly undertaken by men among the Plains tribes. Intermarriage with close kindred was forbidden by Crow law and custom, and the rigorous way of life fostered strength and endurance in children of both sexes. They rarely allied themselves with other tribes for defense purposes and, in fact, fought intermittently with a host of neighboring tribes, including the Cheyenne, Arapaho, Blackfeet, Flathead, and Nez Percé. When the Crow people were finally confined to reservations, their women played an essential part in keeping tribal culture alive – so much so that as recently as 1994, the Crow Nation honored women ranging in age from seventy to more than a hundred with gifts and ceremonials. Among them were elders Marie Pretty Paint, Pera Not Afraid, Agnes Deernose, and Mildred Old Crow – all mothers of their people.

Among the Iroquois, it was believed that the soil would not bear crops unless it was cultivated by women, who also walked through the fields dragging their garments over the ground to enrich the soil. Grandmothers and aunts cared for the younger children, while older girls and women did all the agricultural work, as the men spent months away from their villages in hunting and warfare. At the time of the French and Indian War, Iroquois women were harvesting more than fifteen types of corn and up to sixty varieties of beans, squash, potatoes, nuts, and peppers. Seeds were soaked to hasten germination, and some plants were started inside the longhouses in bark trays filled with soil and sawdust. In every community, a Council of Clan Mothers was responsible for nominating men of their lineage as the sachems (chiefs) who sat on the Grand Council of the Iroquois League. They helped set meeting agendas and actively lobbied to influence votes. Their control of the food supply gave them power over such major decisions as whether or not to wage war and what to do with prisoners, who could be killed as compensation for a slain brother or husband, or adopted to replace kinsmen who had died in battle.

Women in other matrilineal Eastern tribes wielded considerable power as shamans, marriage brokers, and sponsors of male political leaders. However, their principal role was that of gathering and growing food, caring for children, and crafting material goods, including deerskin clothing, woven hampers and storage bags, and birchbark storage boxes sewn together with spruce root. They lived in round or oval wigwams formed by covering a framework of saplings with slabs of bark. These Algonquian-speaking groups, including the Narragansett of present-day Rhode Island, the Mohegan and Pequot of eastern Connecticut, the Montauk of Long Island, and members of the Powhatan Con-

LEFT: Plains women were renowned for their beadwork, as seen on these rifle scabbards of the 1870s by the Sioux (top) and Crow.

federacy were hard pressed by English settlers, a condition that created new opportunities for women to assume leadership positions. From 1656 until the mid-1680s, members of the Pamunkey tribe, part of the old Powhatan Confederacy, were led by Powhatan's descendant Cockacoeske, called by the English Queen Anne. Reportedly, she was a skillful politician and peacemaker, described by one colonist as having "a majestic air."

Women of the original Great Lakes tribes, including the Fox, Illinois, Menominee, Miami, Potawatomi, Sauk, Shawnee, and Winnebago, cultivated corn, squash, and beans and harvested wild rice and other plants for their families' use. They cooked the game brought in by the hunters and fashioned household objects including splint and wicker baskets, cooking vessels, rabbit-fur blankets, and clothing. Great Lakes women were renowned seamstresses, perfecting the technique of ribbon appliqué on men's shirts, dresses, and blankets. Silk ribbons and beads obtained by trade were incorporated into floral and geometric designs, many of them based on the porcupine quillwork that had been done long before the white incursion. This process involved washing and dyeing the quills, which were softened in the mouth and flattened by drawing them through the teeth. They were then employed to decorate clothing and storage bags by a variety of means, including embroidery, weaving, wrapping, and plaiting.

When Great Lakes tribes took to the Plains in pursuit of the buffalo, they brought their quill- and bead-work traditions with them. Among the Sioux and Cheyenne, this work came to be considered sacred, entrusted to women who belonged to special guilds. On the Plains, feathers, especially eagle feathers, with strong spiritual significance, were incorporated into designs for ceremonial regalia including buffalo robes and headdresses.

Other tasks carried out by Plains tribeswomen included fleshing buffalo hides for the tipis they fashioned into portable dwellings, carried on travois of wooden poles that did double duty as frameworks for the tipis. Traditionally, the dwellings were painted by men according to dreams and visions, or to record their prowess in battle. Experienced older women called "lodge makers" supervised the work of stitching together the buffalo hides – up to several dozen of them – for the tipi's outer covering. These were festive occasions, in which women sang together or told stories as they worked. When the tribe moved camp, women dismantled their tipis and set them up again at the new location. Along the Missouri River, women made portable tub-shaped "bullboats" by stretching a buffalo hide over a willow framework.

The primary storage container of the nomadic Plains tribes was the parfleche, made from rawhide shaped while wet and painted with traditional designs. When Plains women painted and beaded clothing for their tribesmen, they used designs representing personal bravery and events of tribal significance. Leatherwork, including horse trappings, was an important accomplishment. Nez Percé women made fringed dresses of tanned hide decorated with beads, bells, fringe, and cowrie shells, and Mojave women of Arizona fashioned shawl-like blue-and-white beaded collars that showed the wearer's status.

Among the Ojibwa, the wife kept the dwelling and controlled all activities within and around it. She wove stalks into mats as floor coverings and outer coverings for the framework of the wigwam, which was then covered by slabs of bark. Ojibwa women often accompanied their husbands to the hunting grounds and butchered the meat there. Sometimes they helped with the fishing as well. They grew few crops except for corn, but maple sugar was an important part of their diet and they supervised its manufacture at temporary sugar camps. They also gathered rice, berries, and other wild plants.

It was atypical, but not unheard of, for an Indian woman to become a warrior. Most women fought only when the men were away and they had to defend children and elders

BELOW: Parfleche (rawhide) containers were decorated by Plains women including the Comanche (top left), Sioux (middle and bottom) and Blackfeet (right).

against a surprise attack. Others accompanied their men on raiding parties primarily to make camp, cook, and nurse the wounded. But in some instances, "manly hearted" women took up arms by choice, leaving their children to the care of relatives while they rode the war trail, often to avenge a kinsman killed in battle. This was the case with the legendary Crow warrior Other Magpie, who volunteered as a scout for the U.S. Cavalry after losing a brother to the Sioux. She took an enemy scalp at Rosebud Creek in 1876, armed only with a knife and a coup stick, just a week before the destruction of Custer's force at the Little Bighorn. As a teenager, the Blackfeet woman known as Elk Hollering in the Water rode with her husband on raids against enemy tribes. Today, female Navajo veterans of World War II, Korea, Vietnam, and Desert Storm celebrate their service at Veterans Day events in Washington, D.C.

Among the many aspects of federal policy that deeply affected the lives of Indian women during the reservation period was the establishment of agency schools on the reservations and some twenty government boarding schools far from home. In a misguided attempt to assimilate reservation dwellers into the dominant culture, children were removed from their families. At the Carlisle Indian School, which opened in Pennsylvania in 1879, Sioux, Pawnee, and Kiowa students were punished for speaking their native languages and dressed in tight, heavy clothing that was unfamiliar to them. The boys were pressed into farm work and the girls had to sew the hated school uniforms, comforting the younger children who cried at night for homesickness. Over a twenty-year period, more than 1,200 students from 79 different tribes attended Carlisle.

Other young women, like Susan La Flesche and her older sister, Susette, the daughters of an Omaha chief (their grandfather was a French trapper), gained strength from the harsh experience of attending schools far from home. Susan enrolled at Virginia's Hampton Normal and Agricultural Institute, founded as a school for black children after the Civil War but opened to Indians in 1878. From there she went to the

ABOVE: An Omaha chief's daughter, Susan La Flesche Picotte became the first Native American woman to earn a medical degree.

Women's Medical College in Philadelphia and became the first Indian woman to be licensed as a physician in the United States. For the rest of her life, she cared for members of her tribe on the Omaha reservation in Nebraska. Her sister Susette attended the reservation's mission school until it closed for lack of funds, then transferred to the Elizabeth Institute for Young Ladies in New Jersey. She, too, returned home, to teach Indian children, until she became a well-known Indian rights activist. These women, and others like them, despite the stress they dealt with in conforming to an alien culture, established lasting friendships that often crossed tribal lines and laid down a foundation for the future pan-Indian movement.

Non-Native histories of the indigenous peoples have focused on American Indian women who assisted European settlers in the interests of their own people, often with tragic results for themselves. The case of Pocahontas (a nickname for Matoaka) is perhaps the best-known example. Legend has it that the daughter of Algonqian chief Powhatan interceded to save the life of the captured Captain John Smith of the Jamestown Colony in 1608. Smith's highly colored account of the episode, published in his *Generall Historie of Virginia* (1624), was avidly romanticized both by the colonists and by the English public. When Pocahontas was captured by Jamestown settlers and held hostage, she became a Christian and married John Rolfe, a settler, in 1614. She accompanied him to England, where she was widely feted as an Indian princess and received at court. In England, she contracted smallpox – one of the many European diseases to which the Indians had no immunity and which would decimate their numbers – and died far from home at the age of twenty-two.

Sacajawea, the Shoshone Indian woman who accompanied the Lewis and Clark expedition to the Pacific in

LEFT: This portrait of Matoaka, known as Pocahontas, was painted shortly before her death.

peoples were to survive. Some did not. Some moved farther west, or merged with more powerful neighbors. Others stayed on as long as they could, surrounded by enemies and seeking alliance with colonists who provided them with guns and other essential goods. This was the case with the Creek Confederacy when the child Cousaponokeesa (Mary Musgrove) was born near present-day Macon, Georgia, in 1700. All her life, she would be a mediator between the colonists, with whom she had ties through her marriage to John Musgrove, Jr., and members of the faltering Creek alliance with the British in Georgia. Not surprisingly, her ancestral claim to 6200 acres of Georgia land reverted to her third white husband, Thomas Bosom-worth, upon her death.

This pattern continued all across the country, as Indian women tried to build bridges to the dominant culture, then found that treaties were not honored and tribal lands were inevitably confiscated or reduced in size. By the early 20th century, it was clear that tribal practices would have to be reinterpreted and revitalized before they vanished entirely. One woman who did a great deal to restore economic security to her people was Tewa potter Maria Martinez, of New Mexico's San Ildefonso Pueblo. The region's thousand-year-old tradition of making beautiful pottery had eroded under the influence of Anglo-American metal cookware and commercial ceramics. Maria had learned the craft from her aunt, Tia Nicolasa, who taught her nieces how to add sand to the clay so that it would not break in the drying process and how to build up the vessel from a flat base with coils of clay. Maria also learned the technique of coating the pot with a wet slip of clay to create a smooth surface and how to fire the earthenware in pits lined with cedarwood and dried cow manure. In addition, she attended school in Santa Fe for several years, learning English and coming into contact with scholars who were exploring ancient Pueblo culture. As a result, she and her husband, Julian Martinez, whom she

1805-06, was another heroine who lost her identity in revisionist history. At the time of her birth, in 1787, French trappers and traders had totally disrupted the traditional Shoshone way of life. Indian men had turned away from subsistence hunting to collect pelts for the all-consuming fur trade, and many women sought to build a bridge between the European and Native communities by marrying traders who came into their territory. Sacajawea was the wife of the expedition's French-Canadian guide, Toussaint Charbonneau.

Cree families often reserved at least one of their daughters to offer in marriage to the traders who dealt with them. Similarly, Creek and Cherokee headmen arranged marriages with the representatives of colonial powers. Through their efforts to reconcile the two cultures – ultimately doomed in the face of white encroachment – many women became legends in their own time at

a high personal cost. They include the Creek Cousaponokeesa (Mary Musgrove), Mohawk Degonwadonti (Molly Brant), and Cherokee Beloved Woman Nanye'Hi (Nancy Ward). They were spokeswomen for the many anonymous Indian women who sought to preserve their traditional way of life through the vast upheaval of three centuries of white colonization and expansion.

By the early 18th century, Indian peoples of the Eastern woodlands were becoming increasingly dependent upon trade with Europeans rather than among themselves. Guns, metal tools, and steel needles began to crowd out traditional goods like bow and arrow, stone tools, and hide clothing. Those tribes that adopted such items began to lose their native technologies, but those who did not were at a military and economic disadvantage. Indian women were among the first to see that there must be some adaptation to foreign cultures if indigenous married in 1904, became involved with an archaeological dig on nearby Pajarito Pueblo and re-created ancient techniques of modeling and painting clay. They also evolved their own style, experimenting with firing methods until they achieved the pottery known as black-on-black, which was soon adopted by other Pueblo potters and painters. By the 1930s, pottery was the economic mainstay of the community, sought by collectors and chronicled by ethnographer Alice Marriott, to whom Maria told her story. Today, the fourth generation of the Martinez family, including sculptor Kathy Sanchez, is still making pottery at San Ildefonso.

A comparable revival in the art of basket weaving was inspired by the Washoe artist Dat-So-La-Lee, born

BELOW: Zitkala-Sa (Gertrude Bonnin) of the Yankton Sioux was a founder of the Pan-Indian movement in the early 1900s.

near Lake Tahoe, Nevada, in 1835. She learned basketry as a child, but did not practice the craft for commercial sale until 1895. Her work was widely admired at the 1919 Arts & Crafts Exposition at St. Louis, and within a few years her baskets were being sold for thousands of dollars.

More recently, Indian women have been forming cooperatives for direct sale of their goods at fair market price. An example is that of the Ramah Navajo Weavers Association, founded in 1984 by 17 women of the Ramah Navajo Reservation in west-central New Mexico. Membership spans five generations, and textiles are made with wool from the Navajo churro sheep, which has a double coat well suited to hand carding and spinning. The women are also experimenting with new breeding programs and improved range management. Other modern-day Navajo weavers of renown include Lillie Touchin, Charlotte Yazzie, Cecilia George, Marian Nez, and Julia Jumbo. Some are combining vegetal and aniline dyes, or working with commercial wool as well as local handspun fabric. Hopi weaver Ramona Sakiestewa has been doing museum-quality work, which she calls "American Southwest Tapestry," for years.

New opportunities have been created by the 29 American Indian colleges that have been founded on or near reservations in 12 Midwestern and Western states since 1968. Many young women are attending these colleges and thereby helping to sustain the languages, customs, and spiritual traditions of their various tribes. At Oglala Lakota College, student Mary Little White Man studies beside her grandmother, Emily Little White Man. Elders serve these colleges as instructors in tribal language, history, oral literature, singing and drumming, quillwork, and basketry. Sometimes they come as consultants and stay on to enroll as students, sought out as mentors by faculty and young people alike.

Tribal arts are well served at Santa Fe's Insititute of American Indian Arts, where talented students from many tribes are prepared for careers in the visual, performing, and literary arts. They study both traditional art forms and contemporary expres-

ABOVE: Nanye'Hi (Nancy Ward) mediated between her Cherokee tribespeople and the white government in the 18th century.

sions, through classes in painting, photography, printmaking, sculpture, creative writing, video production, and other media.

Sometimes traditions are transformed, to adapt to changing times. Northwest Indian College, on the Lummi reservation in Washington State, found it could no longer teach the traditional style of canoe carving of the Coast Salish people, because the old-growth cedar forests that provided the giant trees for the boats are almost depleted. A new class has been developed to study the history, design, and engineering of the traditional cedar dugouts in order to create a fiberglass or cedar-strip version that looks and performs like the old-style canoes.

Native writers like Chickasaw Linda Hogan and Louise Erdrich of North Dakota are bringing new insights to the larger culture on the subject of community and its value to the spirit. As Hogan has written in *A Circle of Nations*, "Like the old redwood forests, when a mother tree falls, a young one springs from its death. I am one of the trees grown out of my grandmother's falling. The line where my grandmother ends and I begin is no line at all."

DAILY LIFE AND WORK

Much of the history of Indian women is written in their artefacts, all of which were imbued with the inspiration and materials drawn from nature. These artefacts vary widely from tribe to tribe and across culture areas, but there are commonalities. Almost all women fashioned containers for gathering and transport, which took the form of baskets, pouches, and bags made from animal hide or woven of such diverse materials as reeds, bark, buffalo hair or mountain-goat hair – whatever was readily at hand. Woven into these objects or painted upon them were symbols and designs from nature that had meaning for the community, ranging from lightning bolts to bear claws.

Women usually took part in constructing the family dwelling, whether permanent, like the adobe cliff-houses of the Southwest, or temporary, like the tipis that accompanied the Plains Indians on their pursuit of the buffalo. Here, too, many skills were involved, whether in making a *wickiup* of reeds or brush, or fleshing and tanning hides that would be sewn together to cover a framework of poles. These activities were commonly done to the accompaniment of traditional prayers, songs, and ceremonials that invoked blessings on the dwelling and its inhabitants.

Sedentary peoples like those of the Southwest pueblos became skillful potters, producing a wide range of earthenware vessels for carrying water, cooking, food preparation, and storage. These skills were passed from mother to daughter, along with traditional means of sewing and decorating clothing for everyday and ceremonial use. Many methods were devised to adorn such clothing and announce the wearer's tribal affiliation and status, ranging from quillwork done with dyed porcupine quills to beadwork in many styles and colors, using materials adapted from traders and placed in tribal perspective. Sashes were made from plant fibers mixed with animal hair, or woven of cotton or wool. The Plateau tribes made bags of corn husks to hold personal effects, while the women of the Great Lakes region eventually adopted trade cloth and ribbon appliqué for pouches and other items of personal adornment.

Tools used for agriculture and seed storage speak of the vital role women played in growing crops for their communities and in harvesting the bounty proferred by nature in the form of roots, seeds, nuts, *wokas* (water lilies), wild rice, berries, cactus fruits, and innumerable other plant products used for food and healing. Charms in various forms were believed to enhance fertility: the Zuñi still fashion squash-blossom necklaces to this purpose, and some women of the Plains tribes wear beaded turtle charms.

Across the spectrum, the story of North American Indian women can be read in those artifacts – some of them still being produced – that chronicle their vital role in the life of the community.

Copyright
1903 By E.S.Curtis

ABOVE: Three White Mountain Apache
horsewomen leading a colt prepare to
fill their water jugs at a stream in this
photograph copyrighted by Edward S.
Curtis in 1903.

OPPOSITE: A kachina doll in the form of a child in a cradleboard, carried and symbolically cared for by Zuñi women who wished to conceive, to show the spirits that they were worthy of motherhood (c. 1895).

ABOVE: Intricately beaded turtle- and lizard-shaped Plains amulets related to safety in childbirth and infancy contained an infant's umbilical cord and were kept as good luck charms. *Left to right from top*, Sioux and Plains lizard amulets, a matching pair of Sioux turtle amulets, Sioux turtle amulet, and Northern Plains amulet in the shape of a miniature tipi bag.

ABOVE: An Oklahoma Kiowa woman in fringed and beaded buckskin with her infant in a deerskin cradleboard.

OPPOSITE: An elegant Arapaho cradle of buckskin on a wooden framework ornamented with colored quillwork. Most cradles had a projecting hood to protect the child's head in case of a fall.

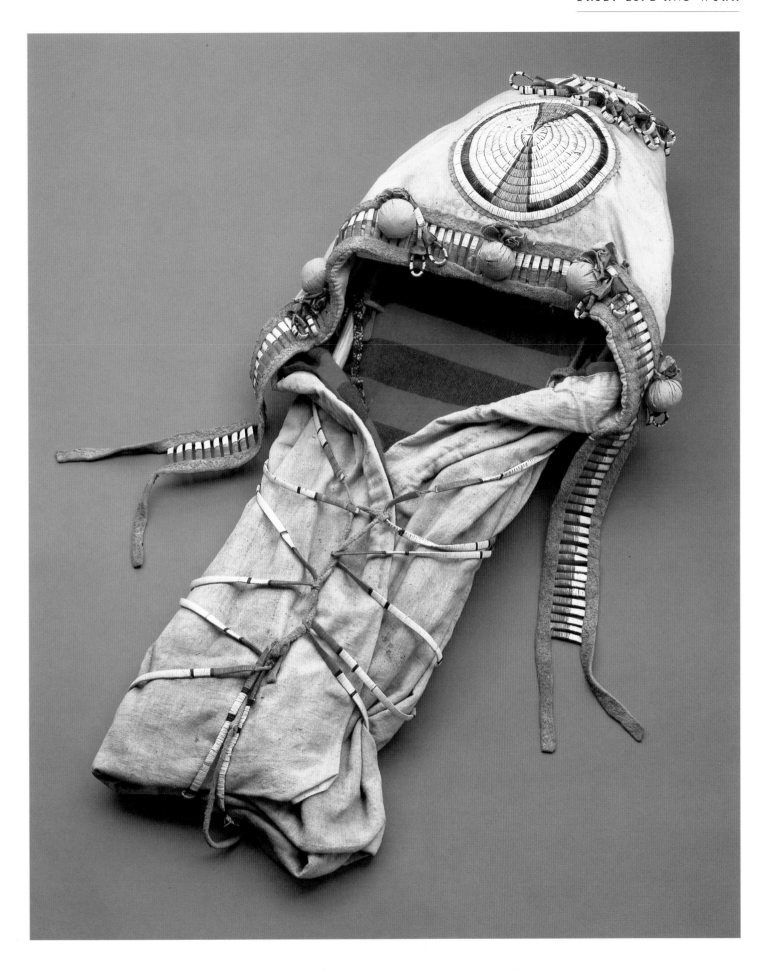

ABOVE: A Navajo double cradleboard and three Pueblo cradleboards, which Southwestern women used to carry children with them when they worked in the fields. Older children either helped with the work or stayed in the care of the elders.

ABOVE: The Inuit (or Eskimo) of Alaska and the Subarctic made beautiful, warm garments of caribou skin richly decorated with fur and beadwork, like this girl's coat.

ABOVE: Sioux women made dolls like these (from the late 1800s) for their children. Materials include tanned hide, cloth purchased from traders, beads, buffalo hair, and human hair.

OPPOSITE: A Sioux toy tipi from the same period is faithful in every detail, from the pole framework to the entrance, which can be pegged shut. Ornaments include beaded rondels, tin cones, and horsehair. Girls used toy tipis to practice the art of constructing and taking down a tipi.

ABOVE: Nineteenth-century artist George Catlin, who made a lifelong study of American Indian folkways, painted this imposing portrait of an Assiniboine family in 1858 from observations made in 1832. The Assiniboine migrated to the Plains from their Great Lakes homeland under pressure from neighboring tribes.

OPPOSITE: A compelling portrait of the Mojave woman Mosa by Edward S. Curtis, who compared her eyes to "those of the fawn in the forest."

ABOVE: The Jicarilla Apache were skilled horsewomen from chilhood, trained to survive on their own in arid country in case of enemy raids on their encampments.

OPPOSITE: The Louisiana Purchase Exposition of 1904, held in St. Louis, showcased the handicrafts of native American women, like the ribbon-appliqué robe worn by this Osage girl. The Osage moved down the Mississippi and Missouri rivers as other tribes, under pressure from white settlement, moved into their ancestral lands.

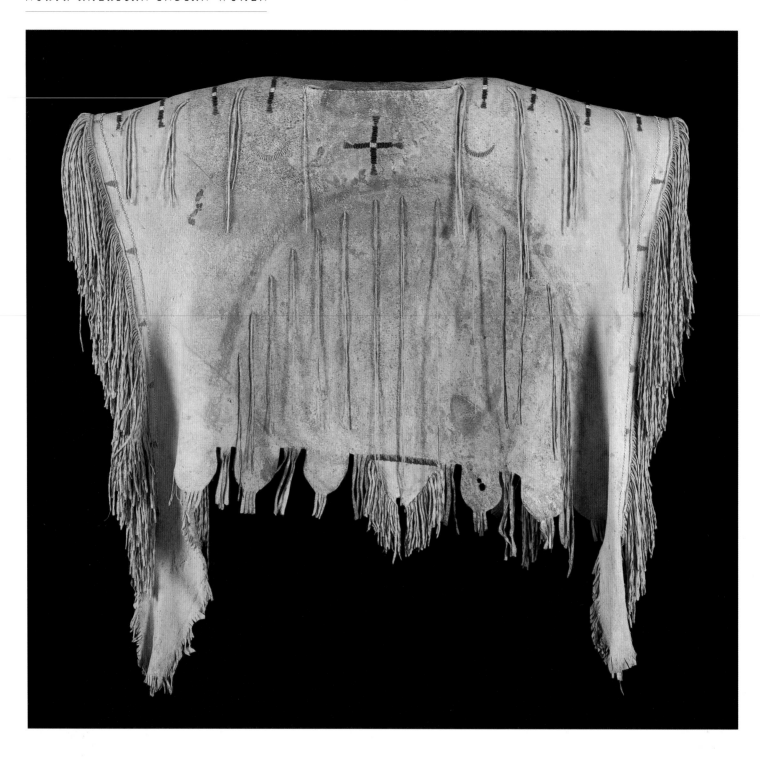

ABOVE: An Apache puberty dress top, worn for the ceremony that celebrated a girl's passage into adulthood. Made of tanned deerhide, it has beaded and painted designs, including a cross, symbolizing the four directions, and two crescent moons.

OPPOSITE: George Catlin painted the Mandan woman Sha-ko-ka (Mint) in ceremonial dress of deerhide, jewelry, and face paint, in 1832. Among the Mandan farmers of the Plains, women were prized as much for their hardiness as for their beauty.

OPPOSITE: A Hopi in bridal costume, traditionally woven by her husband. It consists of two blankets, a white-fringed belt, and white leggings and moccasins. The newly married woman put away this costume until the dance of the Niman Kachina, in the first summer after her marriage. After that it was kept for her burial.

ABOVE: A Hopi kachina manta, woven with symbols including rain clouds, the sun, the eagle, and spirits invoked to confer prosperity in the form of abundant harvests.

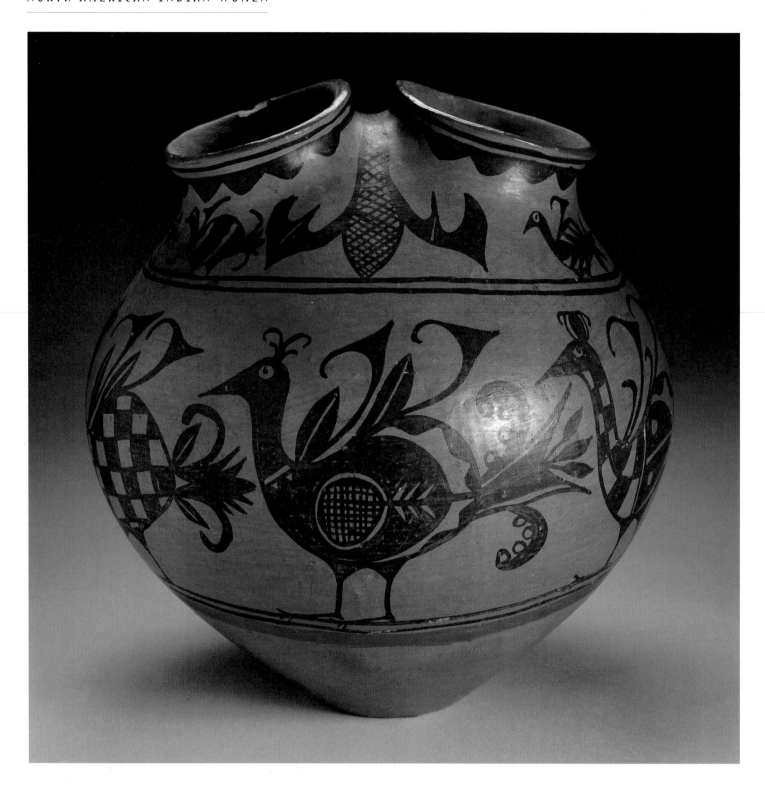

ABOVE: This double-spouted wedding vase from San Ildefonso Pueblo (c. 1910) has the black-on-red bird design commonly used in the tribal style. Serpents and geometric forms also figured on San Ildefonso pottery.

OPPOSITE: A handsome young Seminole couple in colorful patchwork bridal dress, the young woman wearing dozens of strands of freshwater pearls. Photographed in south Florida in 1930.

ABOVE: Tribal gatherings like this one at Glacier National Park in 1910 gave Indian youngsters the opportunity to socialize and play games like this one played with sticks.

OPPOSITE: An Edward S. Curtis photograph of Northwest Coast women gathering reeds for basketmaking along Puget Sound. Aquaculture was important to subsistence in this region of rivers, lakes, and bays.

ABOVE: A hop picker on the Northwest
Coast collects her gatherings in a large
handmade basket. Some 28 tribes
occupied the region from coastal
Alaska to northern California 200 years
ago. Both fishing and gathering were
important means of sustenance.

ABOVE: A Cowichan reed gatherer ties
up the bundle she has collected for the
manufacture of baskets, matting, and
other household equipment in this
Curtis photograph.

ABOVE: Crow women at work drying
meat and tanning hides. Occasionally,
they would join the hunt and help
butcher the meat and carry it back to
camp.

ABOVE: Women of San Juan Pueblo
separate wheat from chaff by the age-
old method of winnowing in this
photograph by Edward Curtis.

ABOVE: Kumeyaay basketmaker Marie
Menas Chappo of Compo, California,
fashioned this coiled basket with a
serpent, frog, and lizard design from
bunch grass, three-leaf sumac, and
devil's claw (1935).

ABOVE: Southwestern Papago women
scrape corn and form it into cakes
outside a cornhusk shelter in this
1916 photograph from the
Smithsonian Institution.

ABOVE: At central New Mexico's Isleta
Pueblo, a woman grinds corn for bread
on the large flat stone called a *metate*
with the hand-held *mano*—a smaller
stone. This method has been used for
more than a thousand years

ABOVE: In this photograph taken in the 1930s, Ojibwa (Chippewa) women lash the upper edges of a canoe, used for transport on the Great Lakes and rivers of the Northeast.

ABOVE: At the Trans Mississippi and International Exposition in Omaha, Nebraska, in 1898, Wichita women demonstrated the construction of a grass lodge of the type widely used for shelter by Indians of the Prairies.

OPPOSITE: The Southern Paiute (Chemehuevi) Martina was known as the Basket Maker of San Ysidro. Her nomadic tribe acquired this skill to facilitate gathering seeds and piñon nuts. Tightly woven baskets coated with pitch were used to carry water.

ABOVE: A contemporary Navajo, wearing traditional turquoise and silver jewelry, weaves a wedding basket that will be used to serve blue corn mash during the celebration.

ABOVE: An Ojibwa of the early 19th century weaves a rush mat with traditional designs on an outdoor loom made of poles. With few exceptions, Indian women made all their household furnishings.

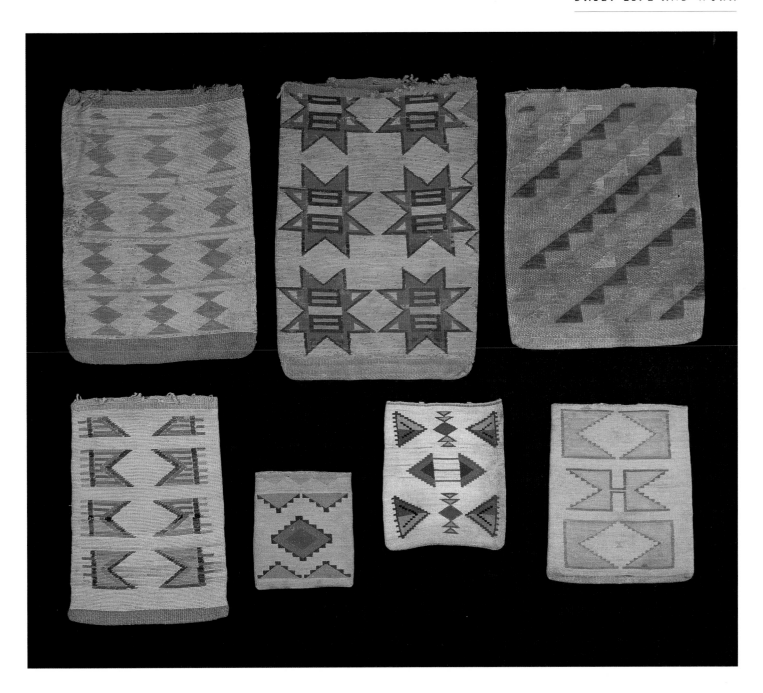

OPPOSITE: A birchbark basket with a floral design in beadwork, made in the 1980s by Margaret Hill of Minnesota's Mille Lacs Indian Reservation. Pliable birchbark was widely used by the Woodland tribes to make various containers.

ABOVE: Nez Percé women of the early 1900s fashioned these cornhusk bags with geometric designs in dyed husk and yarn. The bag at top center bears the Ojo de Dios (Eye of God) design, and the one at lower right has a pattern of stylized diamonds.

LEFT: Pima tribeswomen of southern Arizona were renowned basketmakers who used an ancient coiling technique to make tightly woven baskets like this one (c. 1925) in a nine-inch-diameter open bowl form. The design includes human figures and a bird. Some Pima baskets used for farming were so large that weavers climbed inside to finish the interiors.

LEFT: This Tubatalabal basket (c. 1910) on a willow foundation was coiled with a diamond design of redbud and ornamented with quail topknots.

OPPOSITE: An Ojibwa seamstress fashioned this handsome bandolier bag from cloth and velvet, beads, twill tape, and tassels (c. 1900).

ABOVE: An Eskimo (Inuit) mother and child of Nome, Alaska, photographed about 1915, wear the warm fur clothing made by Arctic women during long winters of near-total darkness.

OPPOSITE: A Coastal Eskimo woman, photographed in 1908, wears a fur parka and the facial tattoos considered a mark of beauty. Extending from the lower lip to the chin, the tattoos were applied in childhood by the painful process of putting a soot-covered needle and thread through the flesh. The object at right is a float made from the bladder of a sea mammal.

EGEDLENA

Copyright 1905
by F.H.Nowell
Nome, Alaska

ABOVE: An intricate sash braided in the Indian Territory of Oklahoma from commercial yarn, with beadwork and tassels.

OPPOSITE: The Winnebago chief's daughter Neloa, photographed in ceremonial dress at the Panama-Pacific International Exposition of 1915. Originally an Eastern Woodlands tribe, the Winnebago were removed to Nebraska in 1835.

ABOVE: These Sioux moccasins of tanned hide are covered with dyed quillwork and bear a bison head design.

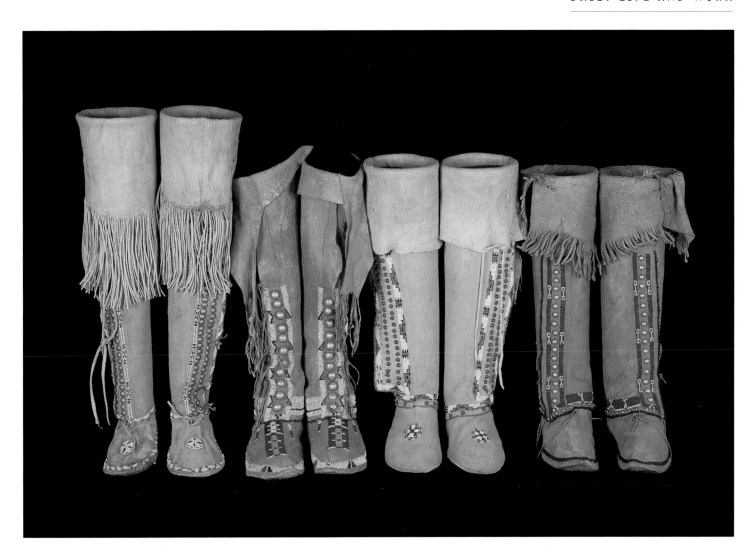

ABOVE: Southern Plains women made boot moccasins to protect their legs from spiny desert plants. The rawhide soles were attached to the tanned hide uppers with sinew. Called "women's boots," they were often painted and decorated with fringe, brass tacks, silver buttons, and beads. Those shown are of Kiowa workmanship, except for the pair second from left, made by a Cheyenne of the late 1800s.

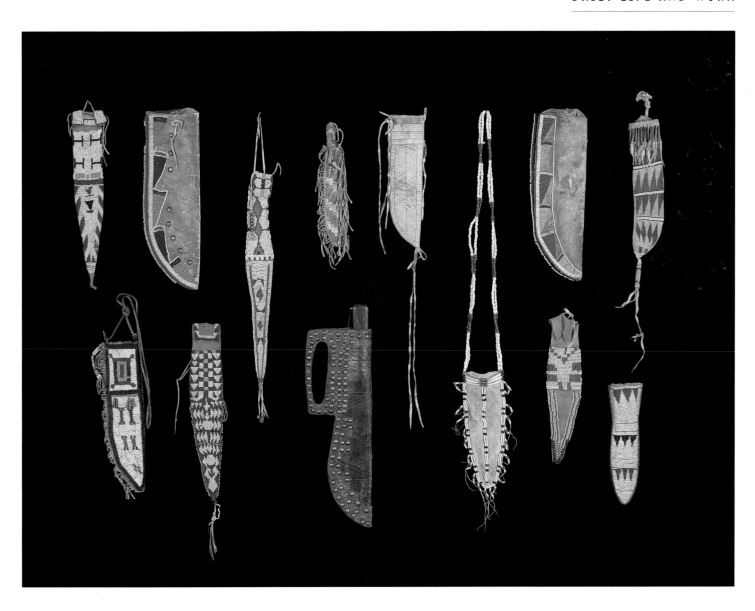

OPPOSITE: A tanned deerhide dress made by a Plateau woman and decorated with fringe and "pony beads" obtained by trade (c. 1870).

ABOVE: A variety of knife cases and belt pouches made by Plains tribeswomen including the Ute, Crow, Sioux, and Cheyenne. Crow knife cases worn by women are seen in the top row, second from left and second from right.

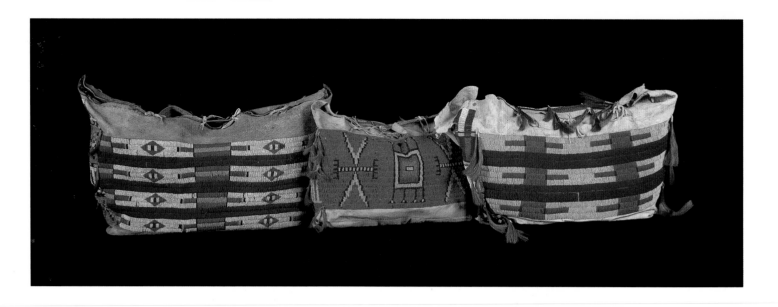

ABOVE: Plains Indian luggage had to be lightweight and sturdy for frequent travel. On the left is a Sioux buffalo hide storage bag with "bar-on-bar" design; a Yankton Sioux created the center bag, beaded hide with the "box-within-box" motif; the Cheyenne bag at right has a fully beaded face with tin cone and horsehair suspensions.

OPPOSITE: This Sioux woman's breastplate for ceremonial use was made of rawhide slats covered with quillwork. Multicolored glass basket beads and a diamond-shaped mirror complete the decoration.

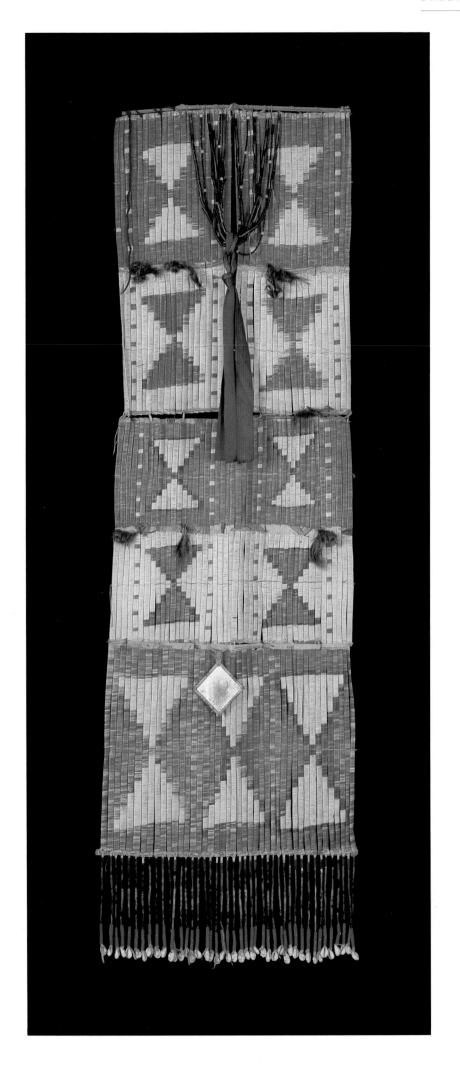

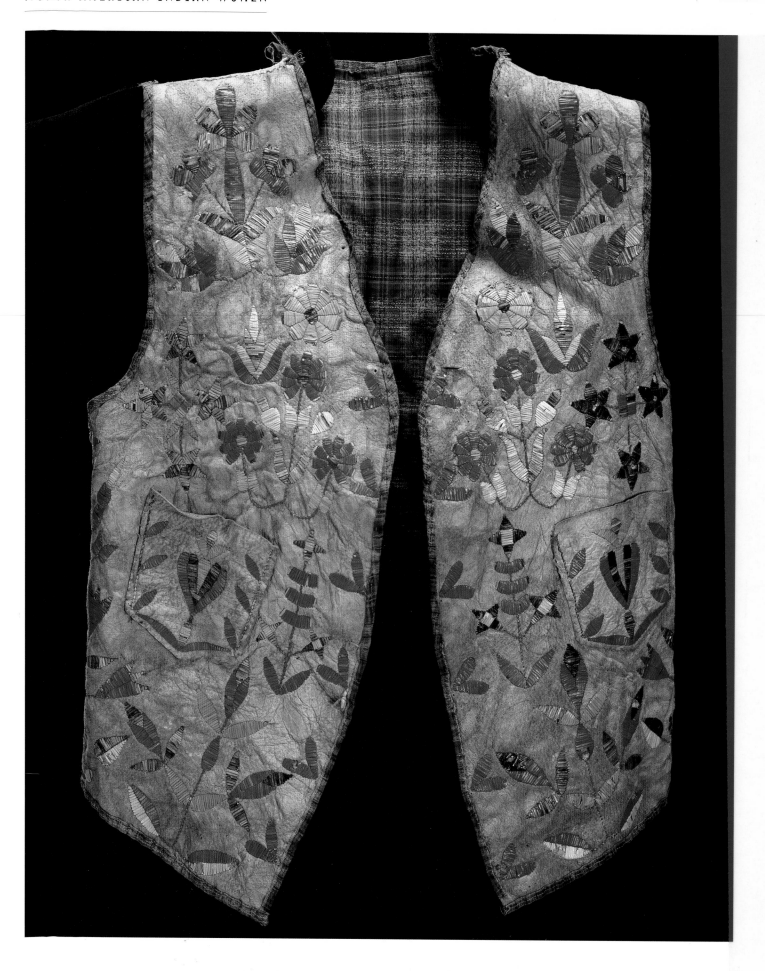

OPPOSITE: A leather vest richly embroidered with dyed porcupine quills in naturalistic flower-and-leaf designs that are unusual in Sioux artifacts.

ABOVE: A contemporary pictorial tapestry by Navajo artist Laverne Nez with domestic and wild animals of the desert and, appropriately, a weaver and her helper.

ABOVE: By the mid-1850s, Navajo wearing blankets were widely used by Southwestern Plainsmen and members of the Intermountain tribes and traded extensively by whites. This Late Classic First-Phase Chief's Blanket (c. 1875–80) is woven of handspun and ravelled red yarn, aniline-dyed, and handspun indigo blue, brown, and white yarn.

OPPOSITE TOP: A Navajo Second-Phase Chief's Blanket of the 1860s, measuring 73 x 47 inches, marks the transition from the traditional banded designs to the more variegated patterns of the late 1800s, as seen by the addition of elongated rectangles.

OPPOSITE BOTTOM: Navajo Late Classic Third-Phase weaving (c. 1870) included diamond shapes with the traditional wide and narrow stripes. This example combines ravelled American flannel purchased from traders with handspun indigo blue and natural white yarn.

Replacement page copied upside down 7-26-00.

OPPOSITE: A Navajo Late Classic Child's Wearing Blanket (c. 1880), 44 x 31 inches, has a complex pattern including diagonals, stripes, and zig-zags in dramatic colors.

ABOVE: A rich contemporary textile in the Teec Nos Pos style by Navajo weaver Irene Holly.

ABOVE: A contemporary Hopi bottle-neck
jar by potter Karen Abeita shows the
intricacy of traditional painted ware
made from light yellow-brown clay.

OPPOSITE: A Santa Clara woman carries
water up to her home in this
photograph from 1923. Purposely
included are the dried peppers and
squash that are still staple
Southwestern foods.

OPPOSITE TOP AND BOTTOM: Renowned Tewa potter Maria Martinez of San Ildefonso Pueblo, New Mexico, demonstrates her technique in this series of pictures from the 1920s, some years after she had renewed the art of pottery in her pueblo. First she wets the clay to a malleable consistency, then kneads it until it is ready to shape.

TOP AND BOTTOM RIGHT: The clay is placed in a handmade mold to form the base, then shaped, fired, and coated with a thin slip of wet clay prior to painting.

OPPOSITE: Maria's husband, Julian Martinez, painted her work with ancestral designs inspired by the pottery unearthed from a nearby archaeological site where he was working, and helped fire the ceramics in an underground kiln.

ABOVE: The Martinezes display the black-on-black ware that became a hallmark of San Ildefonso: matte black decoration on a glossy black background, produced by the rediscovery of an ancient oxidizing technique in the firing process.

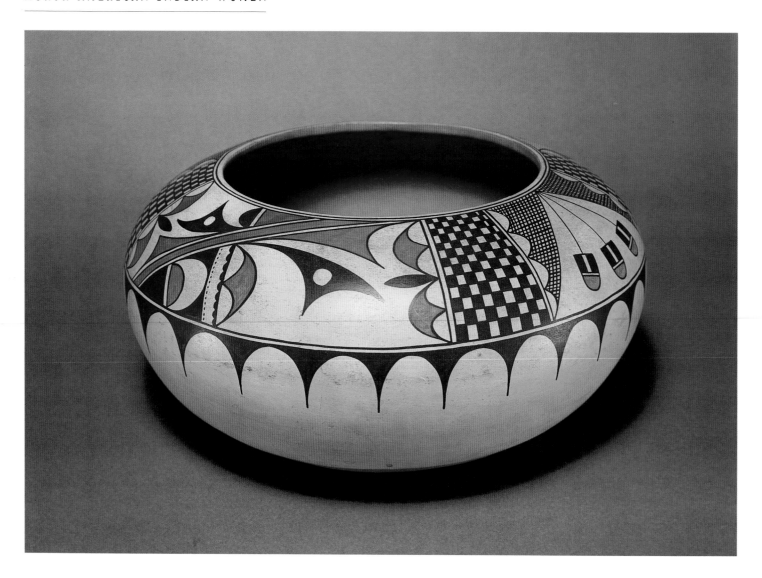

ABOVE: The Martinezes also produced
San Ildefonso's traditional black-on-
cream ware, as seen in this ceremonial
pot used for storing corn, designed by
Julian and made by Maria c. 1910.

ABOVE: The work of several generations of San Ildefonso potters is represented by *(left to right)* black-on-black ware made by Maria and Santana (c. 1948); Maria Poveka (c. 1960); Maria and her son Popovi (c. 1965); and Maria and Julian (c. 1935).

FAMILY, COMMUNITY, SPIRITUALITY

The paradox of American Indian women as seen through the eyes of European explorers and settlers was the strength they achieved through simplicity and what was misperceived as servitude. The misunderstandings imposed by an alien cultural viewpoint made it easy to dismiss – and to exploit – a way of life that could be seen as "barbaric" and "pagan." In fact, Indian women stood in their societies at the center of the great circle of life, both revered and sometimes feared for their capacity to bring forth new life and to harvest the crops and wild produce that sustained the community. Their view of themselves as essentially "part of" rather than "dependent upon" gave them a dignity of bearing and an endurance and strength equal to that of the men they appeared to be "serving."

Those Westerners who came to know the Native cultures more intimately were the first to realize that here was a mutual equality and respect unknown to their own societies, wherein women were, in fact, truly subservient through lack of power, no matter the outward appearance of deference and respect. The demands of a life lived in close harmony with nature had their own rewards in terms of simplicity, community, fair division of labor, communal child rearing, and tradi-

tions that reflected the pervasive sense of the connectedness of all life. As healer, gardener, water bearer, gatherer, keeper of the dwelling, tender of domestic animals, the Indian woman was certain of her place in the world and the honor that accrued to her family and tribe through faithful performance and transmittal of her tasks. The humility of this way of life (from *humilis*, rooted in the earth) could look upon adversity and death itself with equanimity in the certitude that life would go on. All this has little to do with Rousseau's romanticized "noble savage," the concept that Europeans embraced so avidly in the tragic figure of Pocahontas.

Now that Indian women themselves are in the forefront of the movement to restore integrity and viability to their cultural inheritance, there is growing awareness that the dominant culture has much to learn from the one it almost exterminated. Cooperation is replacing conflict along many fronts, as a new generation of Indian women works toward greater unity, harmony, and respect among all "the peoples." Since the early twentieth century, new generations of leaders in many fields have emerged to address the concerns of resurgent Native cultures – repatriation, the preservation of language and archives, contemporary art that

gives new meaning to time-honored traditions, economic security through cooperatives and new sources of revenue, higher education, and unity, as expressed in powwows, councils, and political undertakings. Their names include those of Cherokee Wilma Mankiller, the first woman chief of a major tribe; Kashaya Pomo spiritual leader Essie Parrish; Tewa potter Maria Martinez; Hopi weaver Ramona Sakiestewa; Washoe basketmaker Dat-So-La-Lee; Salish Kootenai Sharon Kinley, Native Studies specialist at Washington's Northwest Indian College; Lakota quiltmaker Laura Takes the Gun; Aleut jewelry maker Denise Wallace; and countless others who fulfill their traditional role of Sustainers of the People in new ways and times.

In the words of North Dakota novelist Louise Erdrich, author of *The Beet Queen*, *Tracks*, and *Love Medicine*: "What makes sense to me is that there is a spiritual life in the landscape, and there's an emotional life around you that includes other forms of life. You may be projecting some of your self into it, but what's wrong with that? That's a Western idea: that you're you and it's it. I think we're connected and however that's expressed, that's part of Native belief; that we are influenced by and influence everything around us, down to the last stone."

ABOVE: Native American culture was on
display at the Panama-Pacific
Exposition of 1915, where Blackfeet
chief Two Guns White Calf and his wife
posed in ceremonial dress.

ABOVE: The Cayuse tribe of the Plateau region was legendary for skill with horses, which were bred, traded, and adorned with horse gear to rival that of the Crows. In the West, the word "Cayuse" became synonymous with the hardy, sure-footed Indian pony.

OPPOSITE: Wooden carving of a Hopi mother and child, 8 inches high, c. 1890. Female fertility was a frequent motif in Hopi art.

ABOVE: A whole calf hide was used to make this girl's beaded robe with the traditional Sioux box-and-border design.

ABOVE: A classic portrait of a Zia water carrier made by Edward S. Curtis. Most of the Southwestern pueblos had been continuously occupied for hundreds of years, and this antiquity comes through clearly in this photograph.

INDIAN AND HIS BRIDE

COPYRIGHT 1908
BY H.J.Kingsbury

ABOVE: A Menominee couple outside their bark house in Wisconsin, the man holding snowshoes used for winter hunting and the woman displaying her basketry (c. 1908).

OPPOSITE: A Papago farmer, whose tribe was among the earliest residents of the Southwest, photographed on the San Xavier (Arizona) Reservation in the early 1900s.

3638. "Home of Mrs. American Horse." visiting squaws at Mrs. A's home in hostile camp. Photo and copyright .91, by Grabill, Deadwood.

ABOVE: The wife of Chief American Horse visits with other women and their children in the pole framework of her tipi (1891).

ABOVE: A Pima elder weaves one of the baskets for which her tribe is famous outside a stick-and-wattle dwelling. The lizard was often a motif in the work of this desert people.

ABOVE: A pictorial by Navajo weaver
Roxanne Nez (c. 1994), made from
commercial wool.

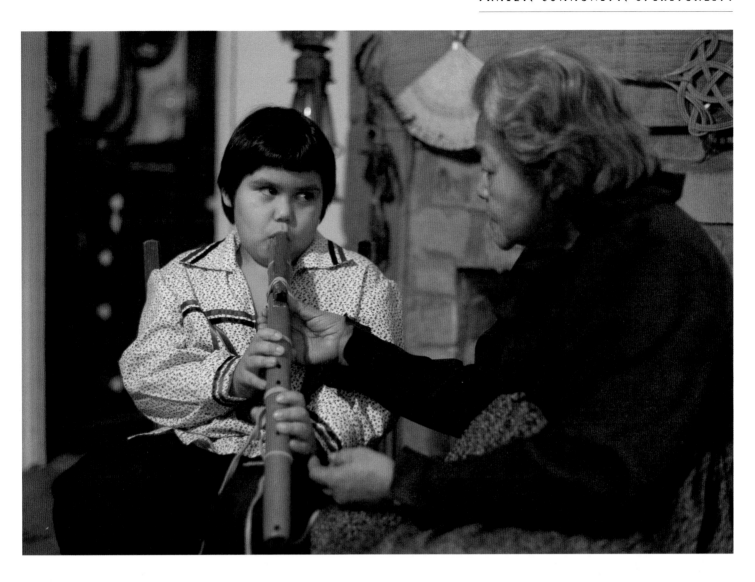

ABOVE: A contemporary Creek grandmother teaches traditional music to her grandson in her role as a sustainer of tribal culture.

ABOVE: Edward S. Curtis photograped
this woman of the Northwestern
Nakoaktok tribe preparing cedar bark
for one of its many uses, including
baskets, blankets, and clothing.

ABOVE: Navajo women often do their weaving outdoors, as seen in this photograph taken in Monument Valley. Their own sheep provide much of the wool employed, which may be colored with commercial dyes or natural dyes from local vegetation.

LEFT: The Mohawk child White Deer was photographed in 1901 at the Indian Congress, Pan-American Exposition, where she was described as an "equestrienne wonder." The Mohawks were members of the powerful Iroquois League.

OPPOSITE: A contemporary child in ceremonial dress shares her cultural heritage at Oklahoma's Red Earth Indian Festival.

ABOVE: The Kwakiutl chieftainess Tlakwéyhi holding the copper plaque that was the most valuable gift a potlatch host could bestow. The Kwakiutls, Haidas, Nootkas, and Bella Coolas used the potlatch to celebrate the heir presumptive to a chief's rank and honors.

OPPOSITE: The formidable-looking eldest daughter of a Nakoaktok chief, described by photographer Edward S. Curtis as enthroned for the potlatch "symbolically supported on the heads of her slaves."

ABOVE: A large Zuñi jar characteristically
decorated with the deer-with-heartline
motif and bird forms.

ABOVE: A Navajo tapestry of the late 1920s entitled "Corn Stalks on a Mesa" made of natural homespun yarns. Corn was a popular symbol of fertility.

ABOVE: An Osage hand blanket of wool, silk, and taffeta, decorated with appliqué ribbonwork, worn by women on ceremonial occasions. The hands symbolize friendship.

OPPOSITE: Sioux sole-beaded moccasins were first made during the early reservation period. They were used for gift-giving and ceremonial purposes. These examples date from c. 1880 to 1890.

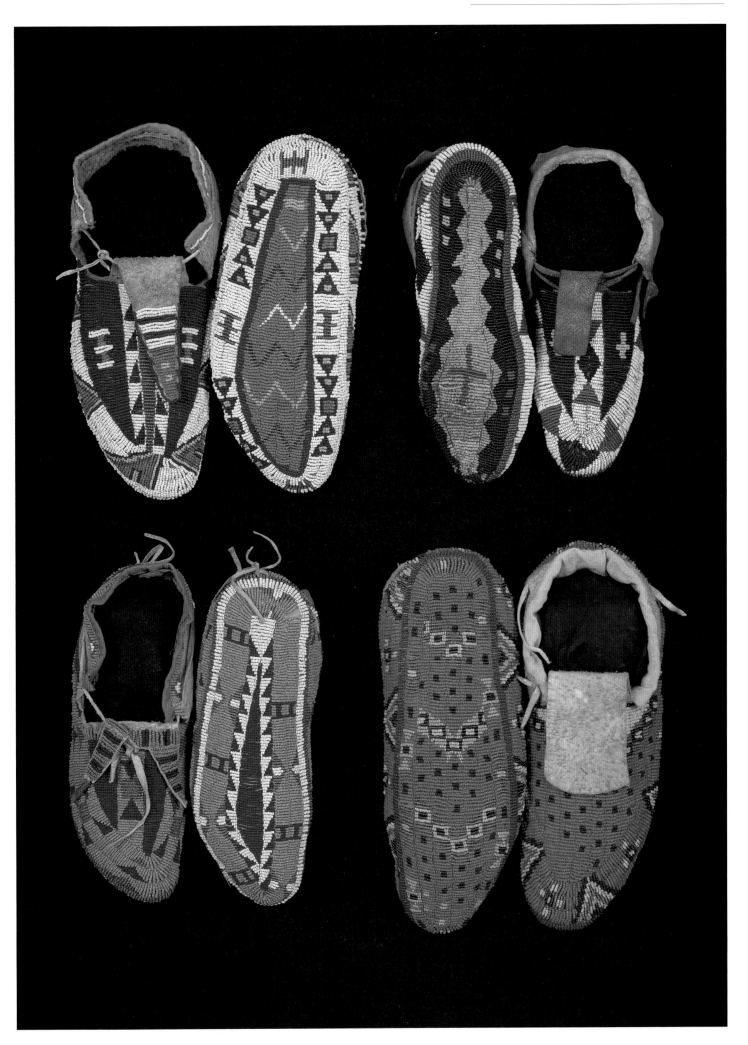

OPPOSITE: An elegant Zuñi squash blossom necklace of turquoise and silver, dating to the mid-20th century.

ABOVE: A Kwakiutl cedar-bark blanket with totemic designs, now in the Smithsonian Institution's National Museum of the American Indian.

ABOVE: The powerful watercolor painting
She Walks with Spirits (c. 1992),
depicting a shaman, by Merlin Little
Thunder, a Southern Cheyenne.

ABOVE: The specially constructed lodge
built by Ojibwa women for the annual
Midé ceremony, photographed at the
White Earth Reservation in 1909.

ABOVE: A Hopi girl in painted and
feathered kachina mask takes part in a
tribal ceremony.

OPPOSITE: A woman shaman of the
Clayoquot tribe, photographed by
Edward S. Curtis in the early 1900s.

OPPOSITE: Santa Clara Pueblo celebrates its feast day with the Rainbow Dancers. The female dancers wear handmade wooden *tablitas* (headdresses).

ABOVE: Arapaho women take part in the Ghost Dance of the early 1890s, which was performed in the hope of restoring the buffalo herds and overcoming the tragic effects of the white incursion.

ABOVE: An Arapaho woman's Ghost
Dance dress made of hide colored by
yellow and green ochre and painted
with dream-inspired symbols in green,
red, and blue.

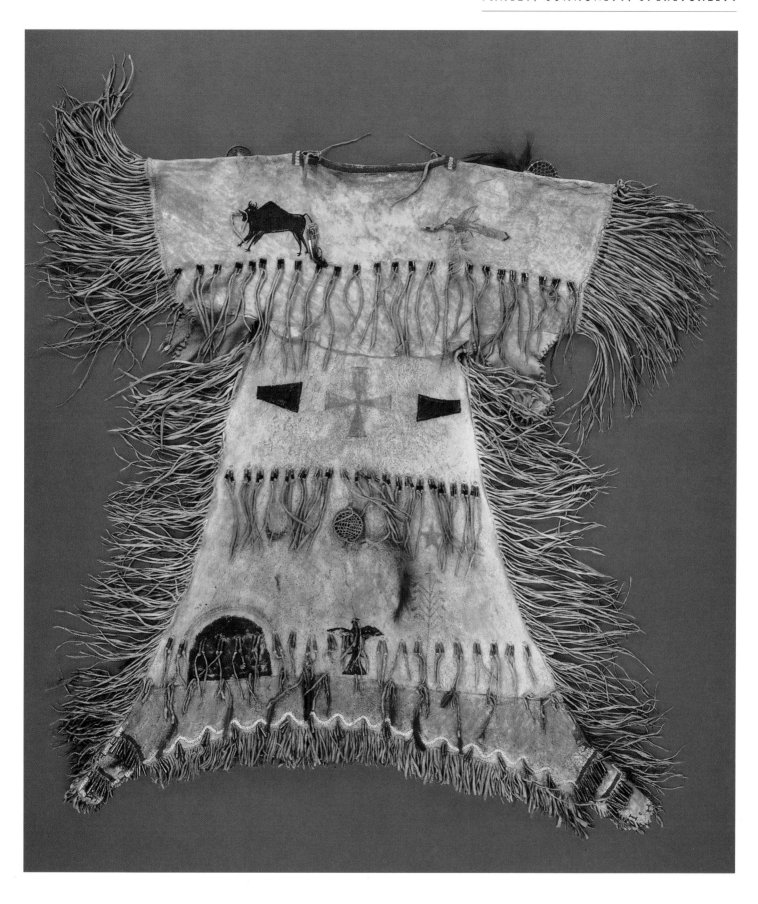

ABOVE: A girl's Ghost Dance dress of fringed hide with painted symbols. The Ghost Dance cult ended in the slaughter at Wounded Knee.

ABOVE: The Apache Dance of the
Adolescents, a puberty rite that
marked an important passage in tribal
life.

ABOVE: A contemporary pictorial entitled
"Yeibichai Dance" by Navajo Shirley
John, c. 1983. The materials are
handspun and commercial wool with
vegetal and aniline dyes.

ABOVE: A Burntwater/Yei tapestry by
Emily Blake, c. 1987, made of
commercial wool with vegetal and
aniline dyes, measuring 48 x 74
inches.

OPPOSITE: An aerial view of a Hopi
women's dance performed in Oraibi,
Arizona, and photographed by John K.
Hillers.

ABOVE: Male and female dancers in feather headdresses prepare for a ceremonial at San Ildefonso Pueblo in this photograph by Ansel Adams.

OPPOSITE: A Wichita man and woman, holding the symbolic corn and pipe given to their people at the beginning of the world, lead a ceremony on the Wichita Reservation in Oklahoma's Indian Territory (1893).

ABOVE: Far-sighted ethnographers of
the late 19th and early 20th century
made a pictorial record of Indian culture
when it was in danger of total
destruction. Here, Choctaw people of
Bayou Lacomb, Louisiana, perform the
traditional Snake Dance.

ABOVE: Eskimo women enact their history and mythology in dance, unlike women of the Northwest Coast, who never took part in the masked dancing that was a male domain.

OPPOSITE: A Zuñi woman wearing massive turquoise jewelry displays her pottery at the Intertribal Ceremonial in Gallup, New Mexico, which has been held for more than 70 years.

ABOVE: A contemporary Seminole elder offers beadwork and colorful ribbon appliqué skirts for sale. Many Native American women keep traditions alive by passing down handiwork techniques to their daughters.

ABOVE: President Ronald Reagan meets
with Wilma Mankiller, right, Principal
Chief of the Cherokee Nation, and
Interior Secretary Donald P. Hodel, in
1988. Mankiller was the first female
chief of a major tribe. She retired in
1994.

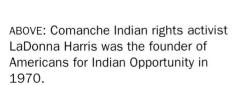

ABOVE: Comanche Indian rights activist LaDonna Harris was the founder of Americans for Indian Opportunity in 1970.

RIGHT: Writer Louise Erdrich, whose most recent book is *The Antelope Wife* (1998), is a powerful presence in contemporary American literature.

ABOVE: Navajo weavers, long an economic mainstay of their people, have recently formed collectives to market their work.

OPPOSITE: Agnes Yazzie wove this Bird Pictorial in which the sacred corn plant rises from a wedding basket to form the Tree of Life (c. 1989).

INDEX